WILDEBEEST

By Melissa Cole
Photographs by Tom and Pat Leeson

BLACKBIRCH®
PRESS

THOMSON
★
GALE™

San Diego • Detroit • New York • San Francisco • Cleveland • New Haven, Conn. • Waterville, Maine • London • Munich

For more information, contact
The Gale Group, Inc.
27500 Drake Rd.
Farmington Hills, MI 48331-3535
Or you can visit our Internet site at http://www.gale.com

Photo Credits: Cover, pages 7, 9, 10, 11, 12, 13, 16-17, 22 © Tom and Pat Leeson Nature Wildlife Photography; back cover, pages 3, 4-5, 17 © CORBIS; page 6 © Corel Corporation; page 8 © George Morris McDonald, CalAcademy Special Collections, California Academy of Sciences; page 14 © Gerald and Buff Corsi, CalAcademy Special Collections, California Academy of Sciences; pages 10-11, 18-19, 20, 21 © McDonald Wildlife Photography

LIBRARY OF CONGRESS CATALOGING-IN-PUBLICATION DATA

Cole, Melissa S.
 Wildebeest / by Melissa S. Cole.
  p. cm. — (Wild Africa series)
Summary: Examines the life of the wildebeest, pointing out differences between the two species, their odd appearance and social nature, and the impact humans have had, and continue to have, on these African bovids.
Includes bibliographical references (p. 24).
 ISBN 1-56711-639-6 (hardback)
 1. Gnus—Juvenile literature. [1. Gnus. 2. Endangered species.] I.
Title.
 QL737.U53 C65 2003
 599.64'59—dc21
                                                          2002006269

Printed in China
10 9 8 7 6 5 4 3 2 1

Contents

Introduction

Wildebeests live on grassy African plains called savannas. They belong to the bovid family. This family includes cows, oxen, sheep, goats, and antelope. There are 2 species of wildebeests: the common wildebeest—also known as the white-bearded, blue, or brindled wildebeest—and the rarer black wildebeest, or white-tailed gnu.

Dutch settlers arrived in South Africa in the early 1800s. They gave wildebeests their name, which means "wild beast." Wildebeests are also called gnus (pronounced "news"). This name comes from an African word that describes the animal's noisy cry, or bellow.

Common wildebeests spend their lives migrating (moving) between Kenya and Tanzania in east Africa. In 1960, there were about 250,000 wildebeests in Africa. Today, there are more than 1.5 million common wildebeests.

Common wildebeests spend most of their time traveling across the African grasslands.

The Wildebeest Body

Wildebeests' bodies look like they are made from different animal parts. They appear to have the back end of an antelope, the front legs of an ox, the mane and tail of a horse, and the horns of a buffalo. Their necks and forelegs are thick and muscular. Their heads are large and square. They have long black tails and dark, bushy manes.

Wildebeests look like they are made up of different animal parts.

Wildebeests have a hump that runs along their back. It slopes down to their slender rear end and thin back legs.

Both males, called bulls, and females, called cows, have smooth, curved horns on top of their heads. The typical horn length for males is 22 to 35 inches (56 to 89 cm) and between 18 and 25 inches 45.7 to 63.5 cm) for females.

Common wildebeests have long, light-colored beards that grow along the lower part of their necks. They also have long tufts of hair that grow out of their nostrils. During the dry season, huge dust clouds may blow across the African plains. These tufts of hair filter dust from the air that wildebeests breathe.

Common wildebeests have light-colored beards. They also have long hairs that grow out of their nostrils.

7

Wildebeests' coats change with the seasons. During cold winter months, wildebeests' hair grows thick and shaggy to keep them warm. When the weather becomes warmer, they shed their winter coats. Their hair becomes short and glossy like a cow's coat. Wildebeests are brindled, or striped. The color of their coats ranges from gray to dark brown.

Wildebeests have cloven hooves. This means their hooves are split down the front. Their hooves are made of a tough, flexible substance called keratin. Strong hooves allow wildebeests to travel long distances without getting sore feet. Wildebeests can run at speeds of more than 25 miles (40.2 km) per hour over uneven and hard-packed ground.

Wildebeests can travel long distances without getting sore feet.

Special Behavior

▲▼▲▼▲▼▲▼▲▼▲▼▲▼▲▼▲▼▲▼▲▼▲▼▲▼▲▼▲▼

Every year, more than a million common wildebeests migrate more than 1,000 miles (1,609 km)through Serengeti National Park. This circular journey—known as the Great Serengeti Migration—begins and ends just outside of the park's border. This is near a dried-up riverbed called Olduvai Gorge. Elephants, buffalo, zebras, antelope, and wildebeests gather in great numbers. They feed on the vegetation brought on by yearly rains.

Wildebeests migrate more than 1,000 miles (1,609 km) each year.

In late May, wildebeests migrate to the center of Serengeti National Park. As the dry season becomes more intense, water holes dry up and grass withers to straw. Wildebeests travel north through bushes and woodlands. They search for food and water. Predators, such as lions, leopards, hyenas, and wild dogs, follow the herd. They prey on wildebeests that are ill or have fallen behind the group.

In August, the herd makes its way to the banks of the Mara River. The animals must cross the muddy, rushing river. Wildebeests blindly leap into the river as they try to stay with the herd. Some wildebeests break their legs as they scramble down the steep riverbanks. They sometimes jump on top of other wildebeests that

Predators, such as hyenas, follow migrating herds. They prey upon wildebeests that fall behind the group.

are already in the water. This pushes them below the surface and can drown them. Crocodiles swarm around the herd—they lunge and snap at the animals as they try to catch and eat them.

Many wildebeests make it to the other side of the river. Here, they find green pastures. In time, they use up this grassland. They have to cross the dangerous river once again, to make their way back to Olduvai Gorge.

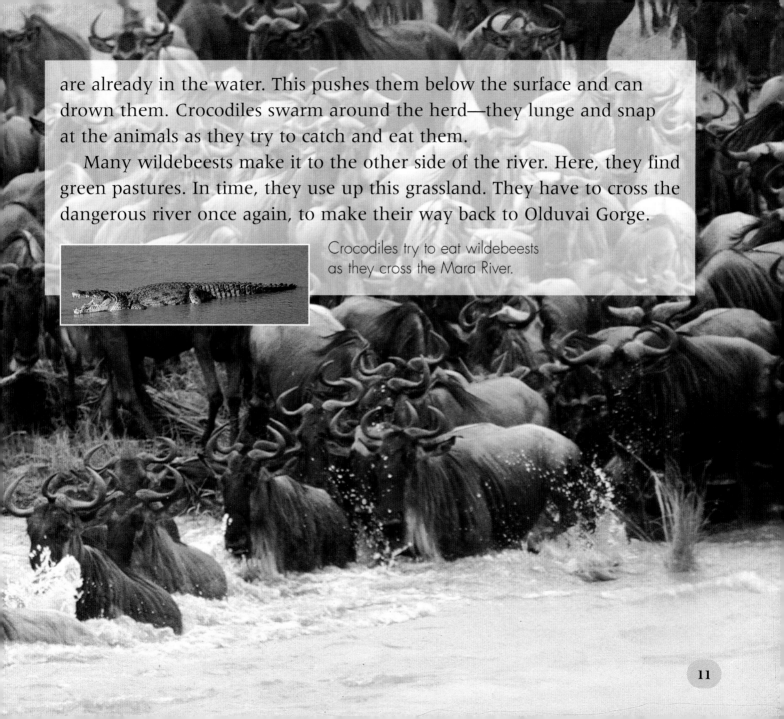

Crocodiles try to eat wildebeests as they cross the Mara River.

Social Life

Wildebeests are social animals. They often form herds with more than 1,000 animals. Within a herd are smaller groups. They all live in the same general area. These smaller groups form their own territories within the larger territory of the herd.

Family groups each consist of 10 to 40 adult females and their calves. One bull leads the group. This bull claims the territory, or home range, that the family group lives on. Bulls have glands near their eyes and hooves.

One bull leads each family group.

These glands release a smell when bulls rub them against the ground. Bulls use this scent to mark their territories. A bull also marks its territory by urinating along its boundaries. He also places a large pile of dung in the center of this area. A bull spends a lot of time rolling around in, and running through, this dung pile. He does this to spread his odor around the territory. When other bulls smell this scent, they know the territory is taken.

A bachelor group contains only male wildebeests. It does not have a definite leader. Bachelor groups live on the edges of family groups' territories. If bachelor groups wander too close to family groups, the bulls that lead family groups chase them away.

Bachelor groups live on the edges of family groups' territories.

Wildebeests often lean against each other to rest. They groom one another with their teeth and horns. This keeps the animals free of dirt, dry skin, and annoying insects. It also helps group members form strong bonds.

At night, wildebeests lie down in rows to sleep. This arrangement gives each animal enough space for it to get up quickly when there is danger. This way they will not trip over another wildebeest.

Wildebeests lean against each other to rest.

Feeding

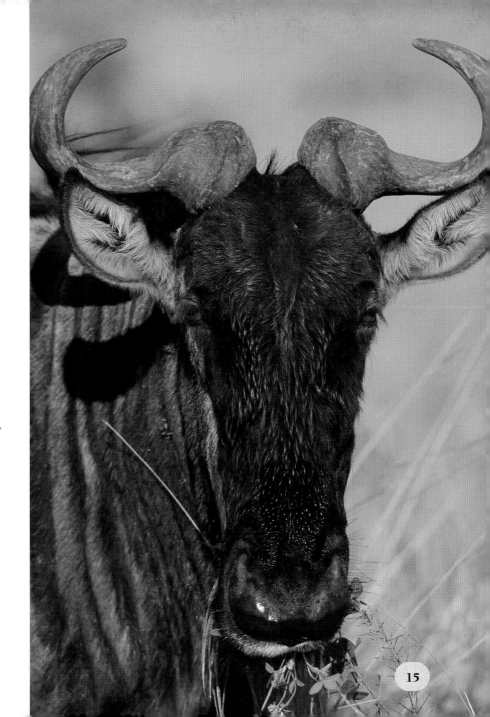

Wildebeests are herbivores, or plant eaters. They graze behind herds of zebras. They eat the short clumps of grass that are left behind after zebras trample over and eat the taller grass. Wildebeests' wide mouths and long, muscular necks allow them to feed comfortably on short grass. Wildebeests must eat large quantities of grass. They feed about 10 to 16 hours a day! They may continue to feed at night if there is enough moonlight to see by.

Wildebeests eat short clumps of grass that zebras leave behind.

Wildebeests chew grass while they rest. They swallow it, then bring up a partially digested ball of food into their mouths. Then they chew the food again. This is called chewing the cud. Wildebeests use their wide, ridged teeth to grind up the tough and stringy ball of grass. Grass is easier to digest when they swallow it a second time.

During the rainy season, wildebeests do not need to drink much water. They get plenty of liquid from juicy grasses. During the dry season, they need to drink water almost every day. Wildebeests instinctively know it is time to begin their long journey north to find green pastures and water.

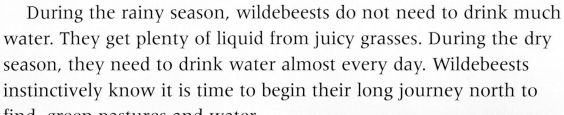

Wildebeests need to drink a lot of water during the dry season.

The Mating Game

Mating season usually begins at the end of the rainy season. This is February through April. Small groups of about 150 animals form within the larger herd to mate. Female wildebeests can mate when they are 2 1/2 years old. Males can mate at 3 to 4 years of age. But they do not usually get the chance until they are older, stronger, and the leader of a family group.

In these small breeding groups, 5 or 6 bulls establish and defend territories that females wander through. Mating bulls have earned the name "clowns of the savanna" because they wildly buck and gallop around their territories. They do this to gain a female's attention. One bull may mate with more than 100 females each mating season!

Adult bulls during mating season are known as the "clowns of the savanna."

Raising Young

Cows have a gestation period, or pregnancy, that lasts about 8 1/2 months. Eighty percent of calves—sometimes up to half a million—are born within a 2- to 3-month period at the start of the rainy season. This increases the chance of survival for individual calves. That is because predators get too full to eat more than a few calves in this short period of time. The timing of the births also ensures that calves will have a few months to grow strong enough for migration.

Cows usually give birth to one calf.

Cows usually give birth to a single calf. They give birth in the middle of the herd. The mother cleans the newborn calf by licking it. This improves the calf's circulation. It also removes birth odors that might attract predators. A calf can stand and run a few minutes after it is born. It immediately begins to follow the first moving object it sees, usually its mother. Calves stay close to their mothers to avoid getting lost or being killed by predators. Within a few days, wildebeest calves can run fast enough to keep up with the rest of the herd.

Sometimes when the herd is resting, calves play together. They buck, gallop, and kick their hooves into the air. They also butt each other with their heads. These games are important because they help calves develop the muscles and coordination they need to survive the herd's yearly migration.

Calves nurse for at least 4 months. When they are a few weeks old, they begin to eat grass in addition to nursing. Calves remain with their mothers until the next year's calf is born. Then, young bulls are driven away by the bull who leads the family group. These young bulls often join a bachelor group until they are strong enough to lead a herd of their own. Female calves usually remain within their mothers' groups.

A calf nurses for at least 4 months.

Wildebeests and Humans

▲▼▲▼▲▼▲▼▲▼▲▼▲▼▲▼▲▼▲▼▲▼▲▼▲▼▲▼▲▼▲▼▲▼▲▼

Every year, people in Africa hunt thousands of wildebeests for their skins and for food. The thick skins are used to make blankets. They are also tanned and made into leather. Despite hunting, common wildebeests are plentiful. They are able to survive in almost any environment. They can be found in nearly every national park and reserve in Africa.

Even though wildebeests are not threatened, the growth of human populations has created problems for them. Human settlements along

Wildebeests are plentiful in Africa.

wildebeests' northern migration route have disrupted their yearly journey. To avoid farms and villages, the herds must travel farther from their established routes. This takes more energy and more food.

Much of the serengeti was protected when the government of Tanzania made it a national park in 1941. Every year, thousands of tourists travel to Africa to see the great migration. With the support of tourism, conservation groups, and the African park service, the African savannas can be preserved. Saving these lands will help wildebeests keep the region as their home.

Black Wildebeests (Connochaetes gnu)

Black wildebeests are black or chocolate-brown in color. They have long, white tails. Their manes stick straight up from their necks, and are white with black tips. They have a dark beard that grows from their lower jaw. Settlers in the 19th century hunted black wildebeests—also called white-tailed gnus—and almost caused them to become extinct. Today, all black wildebeests are descended from animals bred in captivity. They are only found on protected game farms in South Africa. They have the same social structure as common wildebeests. They form both family and bachelor groups within certain territories.

Glossary

Gestation The period of time a female is pregnant.

Groom To clean oneself or another.

Herbivore An animal that only feeds on plants.

Herd A group of similar animals, such as wildebeests.

Migrate To travel long distances, usually in search of food and water.

Predators Animals that hunt other animals for food.

Further Reading

Books

Lindblad, Lisa. *The Serengeti Migration.* NY: Hyperion Books for Children, 1994.

Sargent, Dave. *Willy Wildebeest.* AR: Ozark Publishing, 2001.

Berliner, Franz. *Wildebeest.* NY: Ideal Children's Books, 1991.

Web sites

Wildebeests

http://www.planet-pets.com/plntwldb.htm

Wildebeests

http://www.seaworld.org/AnimalBytes/wildebeestab.html

Index